BEYOND IMAGINATION

Blue Star Woman

Barbara Meister Vitale

To Josephine
with honor and
respect - sisters time
from another
Love
Barbara Meister Vitale
2023

Published by Meta Intelligence Institute
Franklin, NC

Edited and Formatted by
Rhonda Reynolds Murphy

Cover Design by
BlUu Meade

ISBN: 979-888955187-4

DEDICATION

To each person
who has touched my life,
You have made me better.

To Tȟuŋkášila

WOPILA

Rhonda Murphy for editing, formatting, patience, and understanding me. You gave the book life.

BlUu Meade for designing the cover and opening the portal.

Grandpa Dubray for teaching me to love and have big ears.

Joseph Rael, Beautiful Painted Arrow, for sound vibrations, dimensions, and dying.

Willaru Huayta for helping me remember that I came from the stars.

Santee Luke Witt and Matthew D. Campbell Jr. for their Lakota knowledge.

Gratitude to all the indigenous elders who shared their sacred ways.

The Lakota people for keeping their culture and sacred ceremonies.

Pamela Keyser for grounding the stories.

David Busch and Linda Star Wolf for their reviews.

Love to all the many friends and family that read the manuscript and made suggestions.

We are made of stardust.
The Universe resides
within us.
We can look up at the night
and see our path home.
Our journey here
must be told, must be walked.
Live like the brightest star
in all of Creation.

—Santee Luke Witt

INVITATION

This book is part my journey, and part sacred experiences that live through the stories. In the beginning of the book, I share some parts of my childhood. Without you knowing who I am and the perspectives I hold, the stories would have no context. Although setting the stage for each adventure is important, it is the story that is alive. By sharing the stories and the amazing medicine people that I encountered, my hope is that you will recognize the different realities, dimensions, and portals they access.

These stories are born out of indigenous beliefs and culture. The people believe that all of creation is alive, and we are connected to it in many ways. Miracles are a part of their everyday lives. They are one with all of Creation.

Not understanding the language of a culture may lead you to criticize the grammar, the lack of details, and the fact that there are few given names. Fictionalized and generic names like Grandfather, Uncle, or Aunt are used to protect the identity of a person. Name dropping is considered rude and egotistical.

Many non-English languages put the verb first and the noun last. To indigenous people, movement is more important than labeling.

Each spoken and written word has multiple meanings.

Personal intimate details are not shared. They are considered sacred to the person that had the experience.

When I share details, I am telling you how to interpret the experience. Withholding words and descriptions gives you the freedom to fill in the details from your own life stories, or to grow into a new understanding.

Your part in the book is to choose to walk into other dimensions, walk through the portals, or just let the stories dream you.

I invite you to join me in this dream.

What if darkness
was the real light, and
light was what blinded us?
The darkness is the void
and holds all possibilities.
If we are not careful,
the light can dissolve us.
It is within the balance of
these two that Love exists.

—Grandma Barbara

MY LIFE

This is a journey through an extraordinary life full of lessons and adventures. It is my life. I was born in 1937 into an Irish Celtic family as Barbara Ann McNeil. My life, like many, has been a balance between moments of joy, amazement, excitement, pain, and grief.

The first memory I have was volunteering to be born. I was on the other side, aware of the life I had chosen, why I had chosen it, and what my purpose was. I remember standing in a whirling mist of colors. Bursts of light particles flashed in my aura. Beside me was my guardian Angel, who sighed, “You don’t have to do all of this in one lifetime.”

I was feeling extremely excited and ready to make the journey. As I prepared to enter this world, my self-inflated ego reassured the Spirit, “I won’t forget this time.”

Entering my mother's womb was a strange experience. Water surrounded and caressed me. I was not separate from the water, we were as one. My mother's emotions overwhelmed mine. Her trauma felt like a thousand hands reaching out to drown me. As I moved down the birth canal, I felt my brain was being squeezed and all knowledge was falling out. I fought to stay in this warm fluid place. The darkness wrapped around my throat and terror raced throughout my being. I felt fear and the sensation that I was leaving my safe place. I was disappearing. As I was birthed, I came out screaming at the top of my lungs. It was not until years later that I understood that the challenges I was having in this life were lessons I had agreed to.

Years later, after three near death experiences, I came to believe that birth is dying, while death is a re-birth and a going home.

On one of the near death journeys, I felt my ego falling into the void. I went to a place where there was nothing but unconditional Love. It wasn't that I was being loved, or that I was expressing love. There simply was nothing but LOVE. I was like a raindrop in an ocean. I felt complete, a part of something that I had always been. I did not want to return to my physical body or to this lifetime on Earth.

For months there were feelings of loss. Tears would stream down my cheeks until they were swollen. I was grieving.

One day as the sun peeked over the mountains, a voice spoke, “Remember, you volunteered. There are still many experiences that will touch you.” A deep weight lifted from my heart.

* * * *

As a child, I experienced lots of trauma. My mother was schizophrenic and a cocaine-using alcoholic. She was a master of abuse, both verbally and environmentally. The hall closet was her favorite place for punishment. At first it was dark and scary and the walls were closing in getting tighter and smaller. Hands reached out to grab my life. I did not allow it to stay scary. I learned how to leave my body and move to other dimensions. The fairies, dolphins, wolves, eagles, and other beings took me to their wonderful worlds.

It is interesting that I began to look forward to being put in the closet. I would often do things that upset my mother just so she would put me in the closet. It became my safe place.

One day she said, “Let’s make some taffy.” I so wanted to do things with my mother. We put all the ingredients in the pan and stirred until my arms felt like they would fall off. It seemed hours before the taffy was done.

My mother said, "You go play while it cools." I couldn't wait to taste it. When she called that it was done, I went running. In a strange voice, she said, "I put it on the rain barrel to cool. Let's go look." I recognized the strange tone in her voice, but chose to ignore it. I was hanging on to the hope that this time would be different. While I was playing, she had formed the taffy into the shape of dog poop. As we opened the door, I looked down at the taffy. She laughed, "Oh, look! It has turned to shit." I cried and threw up. I have not eaten taffy since.

The comparison between my grandmother and mother taught me early in life to have discernment between darkness and the light. My grandmother saw only Love and Light. My mother experienced only darkness and evil beings. She often acted on their suggestions. One day, she put a bowl of razor blades in front of my baby sister for her to play with. When I noticed my sister's bloody lips and hands, I exploded in anger! I reached for a broom and attacked my mother. By the time I was done, I had broken her arm and several ribs. She never physically touched me again.

She was my greatest teacher. She gave me the gift of being able to see into other worlds. She gave me the gift of strength.

My father was the love of my life. He was perfect! I worshipped him. I was his little girl. He taught me to shoot a gun, drive the tractor, and ski. He loved to have me rub his head. He told me, "It helps my hair grow." My mother abused me whenever I received attention from my father. His job meant he worked long hours. Most of the time, he was not there to protect me.

* * * *

When I was 6 years old, we moved back to live with my grandma. Everything was different. There were flowers, fairies, and trees to climb. No one hit me or yelled at me.

* * * *

During these years we were poor. I can remember starting school with the top of my shoes cut out so my toes wouldn't blister. If I was lucky to get a new pair of shoes, they were two sizes too big, with cotton stuffed in the toes so that I could wear them for two years. Most of my clothes were made from printed feed sacks, or were hand-me-downs. Grandma found wonderful ways to sew them into beautiful skirts and dresses. They always had a big tuck in the skirt, so I could also wear them for two years. I felt so proud of how elegant I looked.

* * * *

I started school when I was six. As I sat at my desk in the classroom, I had a rude awakening! The other children learned to read. I did not. The words jumped and bounced on the page. Today this is called dyslexia. When the teacher called on me, I would look at the page and repeat what the last student had read.

When the teacher talked, I could hear her words, but none of them made sense. They never landed in my brain. When I did speak, the words sometimes came out backwards or scrambled. As an adult it still causes me embarrassment. It is common for me to say things like "coffacuppy" instead of "a cup of coffee."

I did not read until I was in fifth grade. My fifth grade teacher taught me to read. She would have me draw pictures and tell her about them. She wrote down what I said, and had me read it back to her. Once I learned to read, I read everything I could get my hands on. The first book I read was "The Secret Garden."

I often went home crying. My grandma held me in her arms and looked me straight in the eyes, *"You will read when God is done teaching you the other things he wants you to learn."*

* * * *

My grandma was my living angel. She taught me the traditional Irish Celtic ceremonies. She also taught me to see fairies, talk to plants, how to heal, and that I was special. She taught me that I had the power to imagine into reality anything and anyone I desired. My grandmother guided me towards healing and love.

Now in my elder years, the fairies are always around me. Sometimes, I ride dragons. The plants call to me when they need care. They often let me know if they need water. Birds, rabbits, hawks, foxes, and especially the coyotes come to visit.

As my world expanded, I noticed that nature absorbs negative energies and gifts us with inner peace. When I am a part of nature, a true sense of Peace settles within me. Nature whispers truths, is accepting, and gives unconditional Love. As seeds planted in the Spring begin to sprout, grow, and flower, my world is watered and nourished.

* * * *

I was not a healthy child. Whooping cough, measles, chicken pox, and polio ravaged my young body. The only time my mother touched me or showed me any affection was when I was sick. I believed that I had to be sick to be loved. Sometimes when I'm in a loving relationship, I become ill out of fear that the person will leave me. The fear of being loved became a part of me. It took years for me to change that pattern.

Many of our patterns and behaviors come from our childhood. Until we uncover the hidden beliefs and childhood traumas that created these patterns, it is a challenge to heal.

* * * *

When I was twelve years old, I got scarlet fever; my temperature went very high. I felt like my skin was on fire. As I was lying on the couch curled into a fetal position thinking praying and claiming my wellness, I felt a spiritual presence. As long as I can remember, spiritual beings have existed as a part of my reality. Opening both my eyes, Christ was standing beside me.

A brilliant golden light surrounded Him. His divine presence filled the room. He put out His hands and simply said, "You are mine."

From that moment on, those three words have influenced my life. To this day, He and many other expressions of God/Creator guide me.

* * * *

My mother, grandmother, and father were my first teachers. They prepared me for the gift of an incredible life, and the skills to survive that life. By showing me opposites, different perspectives, and other realities, they gave me the gift of being the observer of all life. The many challenges, traumas, and lessons that were a part of my life, led me to believe there were other realities that were more real than this life.

I understood three different perspectives. First, the physical body and its emotions were not who I am. Second, that if I observed life and the many experiences I was having, I could see into several realities and understand their purpose. Finally, if I observed the patterns, frequencies, and essence of any manifestation, I could change it.

I was not just a human being. I was a soul living as a human.

* * * *

When my mother was in the hospital dying, I went to see her. She was so small. The light around her appeared transparent. As I looked down at her, I also looked up, asking, "Will you please forgive my mother? I have forgiven her. I don't want her to suffer anymore."

A very strong voice yelled so loud that the sound shook my body. As the voice spoke, I was stunned into silence, "How dare you forgive her. Get down on your knees and honor her. She volunteered to come here and help train you. She almost lost her soul in the process. She loves you more than you can understand."

Getting louder and more intense, the voice went on, "Forgiveness is a judgment. When you judge someone or something, you are speaking that you think someone has done something wrong to you. Every person that comes into your life is a gift that you have invited. Honor and thank them."

The day the voice spoke to me
was the day I got freedom
from all my childhood traumas.

*Are we ever prepared
to have all beliefs stretched
to the point of shattering?
Are we willing
to be like caterpillars
and dissolve into
nothingness?*

—Grandma Barbara

SOUTH DAKOTA

As a child, I lined up my dolls and taught them about the plants and fairies. It was the start of my love affair with teaching. Having been bullied in grade school, I entered high school thinking, "I will show them." I studied hard, became a cheerleader, homecoming queen, and the teachers' pet.

I achieved my degree and became a teacher of special students. I taught for 20 years. I took what I had learned about my own learning style and how I was teaching, and wrote two books, "Unicorns are Real: A Right-Brained Approach to Learning," and "Free Flight: Celebrating Your Right Brain."

I left my job in the school system and went on the road throughout the United States, South America, and parts of Europe, training teachers. My focus was convincing parents and teachers that these special children did not have learning problems; they simply had a different way of thinking and learning.

* * * *

It was a beautiful day. I had just returned from a weekend seminar on learning styles and brain development. The sales of the book were doing well, and a new book was about to be published.

At the seminars, I met two Native American educators who were looking for money to bring whole brain education to their reservations. For some reason, I was drawn to help them find that money. As I researched the grant money available, I discovered a lot of money in the Department of the Interior. Not knowing where to find these men, I called the Bureau of Indian Affairs and asked for the director. He didn't know these men, but gave me the phone number of his brother, who was the superintendent on one of the Lakota Reservations. I called the number. Little did I know that phone call would change my life.

The first words out of his mouth were, "We know you. We use your book. Will you come and train our teachers?"

I knew nothing about Native Americans, but I was curious. "I would be glad to come."

I had no idea what I was getting myself into.

About a week later, the doctors found a large growth on the side of my neck. They suspected cancer. Having been taught that healing could happen through miracles, I immediately called the reservation and asked the superintendent if they had any medicine men. He replied, "We don't have those anymore."

As the plane landed in Rapid City, I began to cry. They were not tears of sadness, but tears of returning home. I was met by the superintendent, and began confronting culture shock. I had no idea what living on the reservation meant. As I traveled throughout the Pine Ridge and Standing Rock reservations, I was appalled by the poverty. If I had not just gotten off the plane, I would have thought I was in a third world country. Nothing previously had prepared me for what I was seeing, certainly not my education.

I quickly learned that having white skin was not an asset. In their eyes, I was just one more white woman trying to tell them that they did not know what they were doing.

One of my first talks was in Bismarck, North Dakota. It was with a group of teachers who were mostly white. At the back of the auditorium were two Native Americans. After the long workshop, a

Lakota friend, Marge Edwards, *Shoots The Enemy*, wanted me to meet someone and share a dream I had told her about.

We went into a small room to sit with a tall lanky Native American. He gave his name as Arvol Looking Horse. I shared the dream. I am not sure if it was a dream, or a remembering of another time.

I was a very young child standing outside a teepee. It was exquisitely painted. Inside were many grown up people. I knew the Elders were discussing me. When they came out, my mother handed me to an elderly man and his wife. They raised and trained me. (In this lifetime, I met them again. They were the Elders I call *Grandpa* and *Grandma.)*

In the dream, they walked across the rainbow bridge; I became the one that the people came to for medicine. Within the dream, I had a dream. A beautiful Native American woman came to me. She was dressed in white buckskin with a nine-pointed blue star on her chest. She told me to tell the people that those without color on their skin were coming and would harm the people. I stood in the middle of the village and told the people what she had said. The men were angry. They would not believe me.

I went to the hill to pray. Blue Star Woman came again. This time she was insistent. Once again I appeared to the people. Once again they rejected what Blue Star Woman had said.

The men went out to meet the white-skinned ones and fight. I followed, thinking that if I went with them, Blue Star Woman would help them. One of the warriors rode behind me and threw a spear at me. I fell off the horse and died. As I was dying, Blue Star Woman, wičháȟpi tȟó wíŋyaŋ, *appeared to me again. She showed me our Mother Earth from the beginning of time to the year 3000. She said that our Mother would change many times, and the people would experience many challenges, but we would still be here. We had always been here!*

We would learn many things from the white-skinned people. In the future, they would join us, and together we would save the Earth.

Arvol looked at me and said, "It is good." Marge said, "Do you know who that was?" I casually replied, "Wasn't his name Arvol Looking Horse?" She was so excited, "He is the carrier of the White Buffalo Calf Pipe." I just looked at her. "What is the White Buffalo Calf Pipe?" She just shook her head and gave up trying to explain anything to me.

* * * *

Lakota use oral tradition to preserve their legends and stories. The Lakota Nation and others have a 2000-year-old legend of the *White Buffalo Calf Woman*, *Ptesáŋ wiŋyaŋ*.

The people were hungry and had forgotten how to communicate with Creator. They sent two hunters out to bring back a buffalo. As the hunters were walking, they thought they saw a buffalo. When it came closer, they saw it was a woman. One of the men commented that she was the most beautiful woman he had ever seen. He experienced thoughts of lust. The woman motioned to him to come closer. As he touched her, there came a whirlwind and a foggy mist that hid them.

When the mist blew away, all that was left of the man was a pile of bones. The woman told the other hunter to go back to his people and tell them to prepare, for she would come tomorrow to speak to them.

The next day she went to the people. Creator sent the *White Buffalo Calf Woman*, *Ptesáŋ wiŋyaŋ*, to remind the people how to pray. She brought the Calf Pipe, *čhaŋnúŋpa*, for them to use in prayer. She told the people that as long as they prayed with the pipe, they would live. She taught the Lakota seven sacred ceremonies, and the laws of generosity, perseverance, bravery, and wisdom. As she left, she told the people that she would return again to restore harmony, peace, and love to the world.

* * * *

One evening on Pine Ridge as I was talking to parents and elders, the principal asked if I could take a break. I was still under the illusion that I was there to educate the Native people.

I blurted out, “Is it really important? I have a lot to say to the teachers.”

He responded, “The old man is here to see you.”

I looked puzzled. “What old man? I don’t know any old man.”

“The medicine man is here for you.”

Needless to say, I was surprised when this small man walked in wearing blue polyester pants and a long-sleeved white shirt and slippers. I guess I was expecting something more like moccasins, eagle feathers, and buckskin.

Grandpa, as he was called, began by sharing his lineage and explaining that he did nothing. He was only a hollow tube for Spirit, *Tȟuŋkášila*, to work through. Grandpa took out a cigarette lighter and began to move it up and down his arms. I expected him to burn, but to my amazement there was not even a single burn mark. The principal told me to take off all my jewelry, and prepare myself. I never saw the jewelry again. Later I learned when a medicine man or woman heals you, or something good happens to you, you do a giveaway.

Grandpa walked towards me, motioning for me to stretch my hands and arms out. I watched in amazement as he moved the lighter back and forth over my arms. My brain could not comprehend the fact that I was not burning. He put his hands on the tumor and prayed in Lakota. I felt light-headed and in a different place. I was not there. When he removed his hands, the tumor was gone.

I had studied many healing techniques, but none of the metaphysical information or religions showed me anything like this. He had gotten my attention.

He thanked me for allowing him to be a hollow bone for *Tȟuŋkášila*, God. I was speechless, which was unusual for me.

As I continued to share with the parents, I noticed that I could hear all of their thoughts. Colors swirled around each individual. Something had happened to me that I did not understand.

As soon as I got home, I went to see my doctors. The growth was gone. The only comment they could make was that the first test results showing cancer must have been a mistake.

The next morning, still tired from the lecture and the healing, I was awakened very early.

"We are going to visit Grandpa. We are going to do a *Wopila*." It was explained to me that a *Wopila* was a thank you ceremony for the healing that had just happened.

I was more than hungry. I was starving and had images of coffee, eggs, bacon, and toast with lots of butter. Expressing the condition of my stomach, I was informed, "We will eat about seven." Little did I know that meant 7 p.m. It was 5 a.m., and I had never fasted a day in my life.

We drove for miles, arriving at a house near Kyle, South Dakota, on the Pine Ridge Reservation. The house was full. The women were all looking at me as if I did not belong. Although I understood their anger over what the government had done to their people, I had never experienced prejudice. *I felt unclean, unwanted, and alone.*

Behind the house was a small igloo-shaped structure covered with blankets; near it I saw a fire burning. Nothing was explained. The principal told me to listen, watch, and do what I was told. One of the women handed me a towel and a long cotton dress with long sleeves. Not understanding what this structure was used for, the principal told me it was a sweat lodge, or *inípi*. It looked more like a place to roast me.

There was small opening in the blankets that appeared to be a doorway. I watched others crawl through the hole, and I followed. Grandpa was seated by the door; Grandma, his wife, beside him; his brother beside the door; and myself and the principal across from the door. I did not know that was the hottest place to sit.

Grandpa asked for some rocks to be brought in, and as he poured water on the rocks, he began to pray. He asked for more rocks, and the door was shut. It was pitch black except for the rocks.

The darkness reminded me of being locked in closets. I immediately experienced severe claustrophobia. Instant fear struck. Too proud to admit fear, I closed my eyes and imagined a light bulb hanging from the top of the lodge. When Grandpa poured water on the rocks, hot steam began to scald my body and burn my lungs. More panic set in. Grandpa's brother began to beat a drum. The sound of the drum vibrated within my body and I became the drum. Prayers and songs in a language I did not understand lifted me into a place that was new, yet once again I was home. I belonged here.

Grandpa said, "*Mitákuye Oyás'iŋ*" and someone opened the door. "You OK? You want to get out?"

I answered, "I am fine." Many times during the following years, I would say these words, while I was thinking, "What am I doing?"

As the blanket hanging over the door was lowered, the drumming and singing continued. Sitting next to me, "Uncle," as the principal was known, was shaking a rattle in his left hand. Someone or something reached over and put my right hand on top of Uncle's left hand, It then placed its hand on top of mine. There was a hand under my hand, and an unknown hand on top of my hand. The problem was that both were left hands. Someone or something was sitting between or behind us. I glanced behind us and there was no one there. I could feel and see both hands. They were there, it was not my imagination. Dropping into my observing mode, I noticed the top hand was not attached to a body.

Still imagining the light bulb, I really began to pray. Opening my eyes, I experienced the lodge full of bright light. Just as I was beginning to feel safe, *Blue Star Woman* dropped into my body. She was wearing the same white leather dress with a nine-pointed blue star beaded on it. She began to sing. The song was in a language I did not know, but understood. The sounds seemed to come from the universe itself. The song reached out, wrapping around my heart. There was a feeling of joy, love, and peace. Through eternity, I knew her as *Blue Star Woman, wičháȟpi tȟó wíŋyaŋ*.

As we crawled out of the lodge, Grandpa handed me a small hot rock out of the fire pit. "Walk with this and remember this day."

I was not surprised when it did not burn my hand.

Grandpa's brother handed me an eagle feather with small leather bags about the size of a quarter attached. He said, "Here, take this and pray for our children."

Whenever a person hands you a gift, be sure you understand the commitment and obligations it represents. To this day I hold those prayers.

* * * *

One day out of the blue, I got a call from the superintendent. "We want you to come back out and teach some more. Oh, and we are going to have a party for you."

Having been taught by my grandmother, if a person or experience comes into your life, you invited it to come to you, and not to question it. Just do it.

I asked, "What do I bring?"

He responded, "Wear something nice, and bring your credit card." He wasn't kidding.

When I arrived in Rapid City, we went straight to a Walmart. We bought coffee pots, towels, blankets, fold-up chairs, pans, dishes, etc. We then hit the pawn shops, where we bought a number of star quilts. Our last stop was the grocery store, where we purchased oranges, apples, and candy.

By this time, I was exhausted and out of money.

He explained that he had bought a buffalo to feed the people, and there was going to be a powwow where money was needed for prizes. Then there was money for the drums, and gas money for the elders. I was trying to figure out who the party was for. In the native culture, if something good has happened to you or a relative, you have a giveaway, *Wopila*, for the community, and you pay for everything. I was beginning to understand the cultural meaning of *Wopila*.

The party was being held in Little Eagle School gymnasium. When we arrived, there were lots of people. I had no idea what was going on, how I was to behave, or what I was expected to do. The safest thing for me to do was to just observe.

Several elders, speaking in Lakota, gave very long speeches and prayers, motioning towards me. I did not understand what they were saying. I did know that my stomach not only had butterflies, but also a hive of bees flying around inside.

It was time for the powwow. The beat of the drums began, each beat lifted the energy of the room. The dancers came out in their regalia. Although they were magnificent, it was the little children, some as young as three, that touched my heart. The children remembered their ancestors! Everyone was smiling. The dancing was amazing.

I was taken to the center; one of the elders stepped beside me and began to pray and talk again. An eagle feather was tied in my hair, and he said, "This is *Blue Star Woman, wičháȟpi tȟó wíŋyaŋ.*" A star quilt was wrapped around my shoulders and the women paraded me in front of everyone.

Five years later, I attended a ceremony called *Hunka*, or making of a relative. I called the superintendent, and asked, "Hey, that ceremony was just like the ceremony I went through."

He smiled, "We wondered how long it would take you to get that you are now Lakota."

I had become Lakota without even realizing it. With my white skin and red hair, I became a test for many Lakota.

When I get confused or out of my element, I tend to get sarcastic. "So who are my relatives?"

Laughing, he said, "Fifty percent are in jail, and the others need money." He was making a joke. Lakota love to make jokes.

In school we were taught that Native Americans were savages, and ran around in headdresses. The press has led us to believe that today they are all poor and on drugs. Yes, life on the reservations is hard, and there are broken treaties and injustices every day. The real facts are that the Lakota people and indigenous people are human. They are just like you or me. They love their families, like to laugh, love to cook, grieve when someone dies, and practice their culture and beliefs.

* * * *

Over the next few months, my work kept me closer to home. One morning, the phone rang. It was Grandpa, "You come to South Dakota for a vacation. When you get to the airport, call this number. I will send someone to show you how to prepare 405 tobacco ties. Later." The phone went dead.

I had no clue what a tobacco tie was. One sunny crisp morning, there was a knock at the front door. I opened it. Standing there was a Native American man. "I am here to show you how to make tobacco ties."

He took out the red cloth, cut it in small squares, put a pinch of tobacco in each square, and tied it with a piece of twine. He told me to pray for a vision with each tie as I was making it. He got up and walked out and just disappeared. There was no car and he gave no name. I prayed hard with these tobacco ties.

There was no question about going. After all, Grandpa had saved my life. When Grandpa told you to do something, you just did it. No questions asked! No excuses given!

The next hurdle was to tell my best friend and husband. "You are not going alone," was his only response. When I heard the tone of voice he used, I knew not to argue.

We arrived in Rapid City. Planning to call the phone number in the morning, we tried to get a hotel room. We discovered that if we mentioned we were going to the reservation, we became as lepers. The restaurant would not serve us. We were unable to rent a car. We were stunned by the *prejudice!*

We figured out that by keeping our mouths shut, we were able to get a room, and a car from a place called Rent-a-Wreck.

The next morning, we called the phone number. A man answered, "Just take the highway and go until you see a blue Volkswagen on the hill. Later." There is no word for goodbye in Lakota language.

Being a map kind of guy, my husband was really furious. Nonetheless, we took the highway towards the reservation. We drove and drove, and suddenly we spotted a blue Volkswagen on the hill.

We were greeted, and invited into their home. The house was amazing. It was a labyrinth of several rooms. We were led to a large bathroom to change. On the back of the door was a poster of General Custer with several arrows sticking out of him. My husband just looked at me and mumbled, "I think we are in the wrong country."

We were led through the bedroom into the living room. We were sitting in a circle on the floor, sharing a *čhaŋnúŋpa* ceremony. The respected Elder explained that a *čhaŋnúŋpa* is the sacred pipe that you pray with. The bowl represents our Sacred Mother, while the stem represents our Father, *Tȟuŋkášila*.

The only pipe I was familiar with was a peace pipe. They should have named me "Stupid One."

My husband finally asked, "What are we here for?" The elder smiled, "We are going to put her out in the woods, up on the hill, to do a vision quest." Looking very confused my husband asks, "What is a vision quest?"

“We put her out there for four days and nights, until she gets a vision.”

With a look of horror on his face, my husband said, “That is not going to happen! She is not going to do that!”

I immediately responded, “Yes, I am!”

The elder and his wife walked out the door and got in what I was to learn was a rez car. A rez car usually has no fenders, no windshield, and several other parts are missing. As we drove towards the woods, a dog ran in front of the car. I yelled, “Follow that dog!”

Both the elder and his wife began to laugh so hard that they almost fell out of the car. What I thought was a dog was a coyote. In the Lakota ways, the coyote is the trickster. I was to discover that the coyote was a very appropriate symbol for many of the journeys that Grandpa sent me on.

The coyote sat down on top of a small hill. I said, “There is where I am to sit.”

As I stood on that small hill, I put my hands out and thought, “What am I doing here? Am I crazy or what? If I am to do this, show me a sign.”

A monarch butterfly landed in the palm of my hand. At that moment, I knew this was where Spirit wanted me to be.

The elder started laughing, “Come here. I have something for you.” He picked up a small piece of chrome off the ground and handed it to me. It said, “Kamback.” I was stunned! Memories began to flash in front of my eyes of a time long ago when I had sat on this very hill praying for the people and asking for a vision.

As the elder placed small stakes in the four directions and wound the 405 tobacco ties around them, I prepared the area where I was to sit. It was cold and beginning to snow. The elder took pity on me and let me crawl into a sleeping bag. In the meantime, my husband, who had refused to leave me alone, parked just down over the edge of the hill where I could not see him. He slept with his ear out the window so he could hear me scream. The next morning, his ear was frost bitten.

As I crawled into the sleeping bag and curled up, a flock of birds appeared, and they began diving at me, screaming. I thought, “Well, I’ve come this far and I am not going to be scared off by a bunch of silly birds.”

Slipping further down into the sleeping bag, I drifted away to another dimension. It was a sacred place. Once again, I met *Blue Star Woman.* She said she came from the stars. She showed me a star map of the Pleiades. This was her home. A vision appeared before me, and she took me through a portal to a place that took my breath away.

I watched as our cosmic Mother breathed out souls and our cosmic Father formed them into beings to be born on this planet. Watching this gave me an understanding of the balance of male and female energies within all of Creation.

Sometime during the night, I had another surprise. The hair on top of my head began to move. I felt a tongue. A family of three coyotes approached and begun to lick the top of my head.

If you want to learn how to pray, be out in the wilderness with it pouring down rain and nothing between you and a group of coyotes but little red bags of tobacco. I prayed and asked them to let me live. When they left, I drifted into another reality. I felt held in a mist of nothing but pure love.

I began to hear voices pulling me back, and I was surprised to discover I was lying in a puddle of water. I fought to stay where I was, but my husband picked me up and carried me to the car.

The elder said a little yellow bird told him to bring me down.

Near the house was an *inípi*, or sweat lodge. The elder told me to get in and hold the pipe and pray. Picture this, a white woman wearing a rainbow-striped polyester housecoat with a zipper all the way up the front, crawling into a sweat lodge where the steam can get hot enough to burn your skin or melt polyester.

The flies decided to explore my eyes, ears, and mouth. To survive this onslaught, it was easy to unzip the house coat and zip it closed above my head. Auntie looked in to check on me and let out a scream. I guess she thought I had lost my head.

After the sweat, the elder said to my husband and me, "Take a walk with me. I want to show you something." We walked down a small hill. Directly in front of us was a cottonwood tree with many large tobacco prayer ties, *Canli Wahpata*, called flags, tied on its branches.

"That's our family Sundance tree and dance grounds. There has been a big fire that burned most the grassland." He went on, "What do you see?"

My husband said, "None of the grass around the tree has burned. That is not possible!" The elder just smiled and said, "I want to go visit someone."

We all piled in the car and headed out. When we stopped, there was a tall cottonwood tree with many tobacco flags on it. The people were standing in a circle around the tree. Talking to the people was a small elderly man.

Stepping into the circle, I felt a cord attach to me. It pulled me towards the tree. The next thing I knew, I was inside the tree looking out at the people. I felt like a connection between Father Sky and Mother Earth. The power was breathtaking. Something or someone pulled me out of the tree and into my body. I collapsed. Doubled up with laughter, the old man was watching me. It seemed that this would not be the first time I was laughed at.

As we left, we were given a map of sorts and told to meet Grandpa at the Sundance, *Wiwáŋyaŋg Wačípi.* After being lost and given a number of wrong directions, we saw the Sundance. We were stopped at a gate by three very upset looking Native American men. They searched our car and asked if we had any cameras or alcohol. They still would not let us in. I could see Grandpa over by a tent. He had a big smile on his face. He sent someone over, "The old man said to bring them to him."

We were told to put our tent right next to his, and not to walk around alone. There were around 450 Lakota and one white woman with her husband. We had also brought two friends. Dutch was 6 foot 4 inches and retired military security. His wife was small and very much the hippie—clothes and all. We definitely were not Lakota.

By the time our tent was up, it was almost dark. I was very tired. Grandpa motioned to me, "Go over there and sweat." He was a man of few words. Changing into a dress called a sweat dress, I headed for the lodge. A sweat dress is a long dress with sleeves that are at least half way to the elbow. I was to learn later that it was to protect you from the steam, and to respect the spirits.

As I approached the lodge, a woman stepped forward, "What do you want?"

I said, "Grandpa told me to go sweat." Looking at me with anger, she said, "You can't come in. You are white, *wašíču*, and this is for Lakota women only."

I sat down on a nearby log and waited. When the others came out, I walked back to the tent. As I walked in front of Grandpa's tent, where he was sitting, "Why are you back here? I told you to go sweat."

I turned around and went back to the sweat lodge. Once again, they told me I was not welcome. All night long, I walked from the lodge to Grandpa's tent, then back to the lodge. The morning star was in the sky and the sun was beginning to peek over the edge of the hill. After what seemed like hours of walking and sitting, I just could not move any longer. Rejected and exhausted, I crawled into the tent. Putting my head on the pillow, I heard a scratching on the tent door, "Get up! It's time to sweat and dance!"

After a quick sweat, I was told to stand by Grandma and have big ears. As the sun came up, the dancers entered in their regalia. Colors swirled around them. The sound of eagles pierced the air. The drum became a part of Mother Earth's heartbeat. Men and women sang, lifting their voices in gratitude and prayer. Everything became one.

The next day, I lined up to go into the circle. I had no pipe. Grandmother handed me a small pipe and told me to call it a *čhaŋnúŋpa*. Since it was smaller than all the other pipes, I assumed they gave white people smaller pipes. The pipe was Grandma's personal *čhaŋnúŋpa*. I had no idea the honor she had given.

Watching what the others were doing, I tried to do the same. Problem was, when the dancers lifted their feet, I was putting mine down. It felt like the temperature was over 100 degrees. Around noon, Grandpa called me over, "You OK? Maybe you should stop."

Not wanting to show weakness, "I am OK."

The next thing I knew, I was in real trouble. I could see a white tunnel, and knew I was going to black out. I asked the head woman dancer if I could stop dancing. It was obvious she saw me as white, did not like me, and felt I should not be dancing. "You have to go ask the old man."

I could not stand, so with everyone watching, I crawled towards Grandpa. I looked up at him and said, "I need to stop dancing." Smiling, he just said, "No! You came in here to remember who you are. You can leave the dance and never come back to the reservation." He went on, "It is a good day to die and we will honor you. Or you can go back in that dance and remember."

I could not stand up to leave. I didn't want to die. My only option was to let them carry me to the women's teepee to be doctored. Their method of doctoring was to tell me I was white, how weak I was, and how I was hurting the other dancers.

At that point, I would have done anything to get away from these women. I managed to stand up and walk towards the arbor. The woman who had helped me make a sage crown and wristlets, that you wear to protect yourself, walked up to me and said, "Here, you dance with this. It will help you." She handed me a beat-up bird wing with red cloth wrapped around the bottom. When I held it, it felt like I was becoming an eagle. I later found out it was an eagle fan that had been gifted to her by her grandfather, Fools Crow.

As I danced, I was flying with the Eagles. I became the eagle. The sun danced me. As I looked at the sun, I went through it to a black sun. On the other side of the black sun, *Blue Star Woman* was waiting for me. Her smile touched creation, surrounding me with light. She reached out and wrapped me in peace. Once again, she took me home.

At the end of the day, Grandpa gave a quirky half smile, "You're done. You remembered who your ancestors are. You owed me one day from that other time."

For many years, I presented him the pipe, *čhaŋnúŋpa*, to dance. Each time he said, "You take care of Auntie and the people. That's your reason." Like my mother, Auntie was a two-faced sacred being.

A few years later, before Sundance, *Wiwáŋyaŋg Wačípi*, started, a man angry that Grandpa had white people dancing, pointed a gun at Grandpa's head. The Sundancers wanted to take him down. Instead, Grandpa told them to forgive this man. Grandpa told all of us to feed him and thank him for teaching us about our anger and lack of forgiveness.

After the dance, my husband and I were directed to go back to the elder that had put me on the hill. When we arrived, I was presented with an elk *čhaŋnúŋpa*. "Go home and pray. Try to figure out what just happened to you. Then come back."

Something on a small hill was calling to me. Lying on the ground was a coyote skull. I picked it up to take home. My husband glared at me and just said, "No!" They will think we have killed someone. We will be arrested when we try and take it on the plane."

It didn't matter. The coyote had become a spirit helper for me. The coyote had tricked me into becoming Lakota and walking the Red Road for the rest of my life.

When I got home, I could not read enough books on the meanings of all that had happened. What I did not realize was it was just starting.

* * * *

Each year, I went to South Dakota. First to Bear Butte to help with the vision quests, then later in the summer to the Sundance, *Wiwáŋyaŋg Wačípi.*

The Lakota call Bear Butte, *Mathˇó Pahá*. Many Native Americans visit this ceremonial area each summer. The mountain is sacred to many indigenous peoples. It is a place where *Thˇuŋkášila* and the Ancestors communicate with the people through visions and prayers. Bear Butte is a sacred place. It is also a place where challenging lessons are taught.

It was a beautiful morning. Grandpa was calling everyone to the sweat, "You women take that path to change."

The path was narrow, and both sides were covered with poison oak. Having learned from my grandmother, I began to talk to the plants and ask their permission to enter. Walking with respect, the way was opened. When I came out dressed in a sweat dress, Grandpa looked at me, "Why are you dressed like that. Go get some clothes on."

I turned and went back down the path, and changed into my denim dress with large metal buttons, a heavy denim apron, and warm tights.

Just as I exited the path, Grandpa said, "I thought I told you to get ready for the sweat lodge."

We did this dance several times. The plants were getting less tolerant. As I slipped out wearing my full denim armor, I hid over the edge of the hill so Grandpa couldn't see me. Sitting there praying, I heard, "You down there. Your ears aren't big enough yet. In the lodge like that."

Those who have been in a sweat lodge, *inípi*, or even a sauna know that denim is not a wise choice. Since heat rises, lying on the ground seemed safer.

"You are being disrespectful. Sit up. Honor your ancestors. You take this dipper and pour."

"I am not ready." This was the last time I ever said that to Grandpa or any other elder.

My ears seemed to grow slowly. Throughout the years, it seemed that I was yelled at for everything, and everything everyone else did.

One night when it had been a particularly hard day, I went to Grandma with tears streaming down my face and asked, "Why does Grandpa treat me this way?"

She put her arms around me, "Because you're worth it."

It took me many years to understand the tests I was being put through. There are no shortcuts.

Some years, it would snow at Bear Butte in June. One year, it was exceptionally cold and wet. Several were there to do vision quests to prepare for Sundance, *Wiwáŋyaŋg Wačípi*. Although I had a very sore throat, I had decided to go anyway. As it got colder, Grandpa whispered to me, "Go into town and get two hotel rooms; one for Grandma and me, one for Uncle, and get one for yourself."

Leaving, I handed my boots, extra coat, and all the blankets that were in the car out the window for those going on the hill.

As soon as I left, Grandpa told everyone, "She is not Lakota. She is not strong. You are the strong ones. She has dishonored the Spirits."

In the meantime, I went into town and paid for three rooms. Grandpa never showed up. I called all the hotels and motels in the town. He was at one across the street. The motel was waiting for me to pay for the rooms. Finding Grandpa in the new room, I asked, "What was wrong with the first motel?"

Looking me straight in the eye, "They don't like Indians."

I had given the first hotel a list of names that might need rooms. I told the manager to give the extra rooms to anyone on the list that came in. There were some that were warm that night.

The next morning, we drove back out to Bear Butte. There were several people standing at the small bridge we had to cross. One of them said, "You can't come over the bridge. You dishonored the Spirits."

Grandpa was just watching and smiling. When he was having fun, he had this lip that went up in a half smile. I called it his quirky smile. At that point, I had no idea what he had said to them or why they were acting this way. He motioned for them to bring me to him. "Sometimes we use some to motivate others. Thanks for the motel room."

Over the years, he used me many times in this way. If someone was doing something wrong and I was doing it as he or Grandma had taught me, he would scold me for doing it wrong. It took many years and many tears before understanding this. Each time he would say, "*Pilamayaye*," thank you.

Over time, Grandpa taught me not to take things personally, that sometimes things were backwards, that the energy must be in balance, that the ways of the ancestors were to be honored, and to keep love and forgiveness in my heart.

The weather on Bear Butte was unpredictable. During vision quests, it seemed to rain and sometimes snow. There was a big rainstorm coming. Grandpa motioned, "Get me a big glass of water." As I handed it to him, he held the glass up towards the storm and prayed. It was as if the storm talked back. He raised the glass and drank every drop of water. As I watched, the storm split in half, and moved around the butte. He gave me his quirky smile and said, "Did you get that one?"

There was medicine and magic at Bear Butte, but the Sundance, *Wiwáŋyaŋg Wačípi*, took it to a higher sacred level.

Each morning just as the sun peeked over the horizon, the dancers would enter the Sundance grounds to pray for the people. Grandpa led the procession, followed by the buffalo skull, a young virgin girl carrying the *čhaŋnúŋpa*, and the dancers. Behind these were all the ancestors that had dropped their robes, their human bodies, and existed on the other side. Sometimes the Sundance leader comes in last.

A storm raced across the prairie. Menacing gray clouds rolled across the sky. As the clouds broke open, torrents of rain and hail fell from the sky. All the Sundancers ran for their tents and teepees. Grandpa stood alone welcoming the Thunder Beings. Lightning flashed all around the Sundance tree. Transfixed by the power of the energy, I was unable to move. Grandpa was dancing with the Thunder Beings and praying. Then he was gone. In his place was a brilliant multi-colored egg. Colors weaved possibilities. Light danced and shimmered, calling to the storm. Suddenly, the storm stopped. The Thunder Beings had heard his prayer.

* * * *

Although Grandpa had told me to stick to the Lakota way, I would sometimes slip off to learn from other medicine people. My cell phone rang. *Beautiful Painted Arrow*, Joseph Rael, was on the phone. "I want you to come to my place."

"Why am I coming?"

I could hear laughter in his voice, "I will tell you when you get here."

When I arrived, I asked him again why I was there. "To learn how to die." After being given some sacred medicine, I found myself floating above my body. I had fought leaving my body. In fact, I remember that someone pulled me out through a tunnel or very big straw. As I looked back at my body, it appeared empty. I tried to get back in, but the door had been shut. As the portals within this ceremony opened, I became in awe of dying. I lost all fear of death.

I was also in gratitude of being pulled back to life on Earth. I enjoy watching the sunrise and sunset, talking with animals, breathing, counting the stars in the sky, smelling the air after a summer rainstorm, family and friends, loving everything, and of course chocolate.

Before you do a ceremony, make sure the person leading the ceremony has not learned it by reading a book. Training for ceremonies takes many years. Those leading the ceremony must dream it, have specific Spirits come to them, and take it to the elders.

* * * *

I collect pots, paintings, and sacred objects to remember the energies of experiences. On the way to the Phoenix airport, we passed a small tourist shop. Their windows were full of native pots. Most of the pots were made in China for tourists. I wasn't sure why I felt the need to stop. Sometimes the pull to do something and your knowingness override logical action. As I entered the store, I got goose bumps. I asked the clerk if she had any traditional Tiwa pots. She looked at me for a moment. "You know I think we have one that has been here for a very long time."

Disappearing into the back storage room, she reappeared holding a small pot made of mica clay. It was just what I was imagining. I asked, "Do you know who the artist is?"

"No, I don't have any idea."

I turned the pot over. On the bottom was the name of the artist, J. Dubray. Grandpa's name was James Dubray.

Several months later, he and Grandma came to visit. Usually when they arrive, Grandpa would shake hands and say hello. This time, as I opened the door, he walked right past me into the living room where I had put the pot. He just stood there and laughed. "Did you enjoy dying?"

He went on to say that he had made it when he was studying art in college. I don't believe this was a random happening.

Over the years, wherever I traveled to learn from medicine people, his name would always come up. There is a connection between those that know and walk a deep spiritual path.

* * * *

Every year, just before Sundance, *Wiwáŋyaŋg Wačípi*, several of us would go to South Dakota to help with preparations. We were invited to stay in Grandpa and Grandma's house. There were people sleeping on every mattress, couch, and space on the floor that was vacant. One year I was staying in a small bedroom at the end of the hallway. It was about three or four a.m. I woke up needing to walk down the hall to the bathroom. I quietly opened the door. Grandpa was walking down the hall. A tall man with a middle-eastern skin color was walking in front of him. He was wearing a long off-white robe and sandals. His hair was brown and hung to his shoulders. Surrounding him was a bright white light. He seemed to float. He was as real as Grandpa.

I quickly closed the door and crawled out the window to the outhouse. The next morning I asked Grandpa, "Was that man who I think he was?"

"Yep! He comes to visit me often."

I was no longer surprised at anything I saw, heard, or experienced when I was around Grandpa.

* * * *

One year at powwow, to celebrate his and Grandma's anniversary, Grandpa had volunteered to feed the people. There were a few hundred people. The family had just put large chunks of meat in the kettles over open fires. In the kitchen, some of the women were beginning to cook side dishes. The feast was to be around suppertime.

Around noon, Grandpa came to the screen door and motioned to me. "Granddaughter, there is no one to feed the people. We are going to feed in 15 minutes."

I opened my mouth to say something, when he cut me off, "You be there."

I turned around and looked at the women. "Stop whatever you are doing. We are feeding in 15 minutes." One woman opened her mouth to say something. I just looked at her, "Just move. Now."

We had a large pot of soup, six watermelons, seven loaves of bread, and one big bowl of fruit cocktail. More people had arrived. The helpers served all of the people, and even filled the coffee cans that elders had brought to take home.

When we were done, there were about 2 inches of soup left, a little bit of fruit cocktail, one uncut watermelon, and one unopened loaf of bread.

Grandpa smiled, "That man that visits me fed the people with five loaves and two fish. That water became wine. He told us you can do greater things than I do."

Sometimes there is
a thin veil between
the present moment and
portals into other lives,
dimensions, and the soul.
Is your mind creating
your reality, or is reality
creating your mind?

—Grandma Barbara

MEXICO

Since I had quit my job, I was looking forward to taking a vacation. As I looked at the mail, I noticed that there was an envelope with no return address. Inside was a ticket for two people to any place in the world. I called my friend Bella.

We had met a group of Aztec dancers at a small metaphysical store in Florida. Bella had become very good friends with several in the dance troupe. I knew she wanted to go to Mexico.

When she answered the phone and I told her about the ticket, "When do we leave?"

The next few days, I made hotel reservations and booked flights to the ancient Mayan city of Palenque.

The flight was to be direct from Miami to Mexico City. At the very last minute, the airline informed us that we were taking a different route.

It was a much longer route that took us across the country to Los Angeles, City of Angels, and then to Mexico City. As we were in the air, I looked out the window. "Bella, look out the window. What is that?" We both saw a round shiny disc flying beside the airplane.

We called the flight attendant, "What is that?" She looked out the window, "I don't see anything." After she walked away, Bella and I just started laughing. This was definitely not going to be an ordinary vacation.

Walking off the plane in Mexico City, we were greeted by the Aztec dancers. I asked where we could get the hotel shuttle. The lead dancer smiled, "We have canceled your hotel and flights. We want you to stay with us, unless you think we are too poor. I will drive you where you want to go." How does anyone respond to this without offending?

A weird feeling about what was going to occur edged its way into my consciousness. I chose to ignore the feeling. Something was happening, but I did not know what it was. What I did know was that Spirit was in charge!

We all piled into their truck and headed to their home. It was an alley house. Let me see if I can explain this house. It was actually built in a wide alley. Along one side of the alley were all the rooms. There were no doors joining them. The only way you could get from one room to another was to go outside. The kitchen was outside against the opposite stone wall.

We were given a new room that they had just finished. As tradition demanded, we were given the best, including a beautiful new bedspread.

I had hired an interpreter out of an art community in Mexico. I had given her the address, but she got lost. When she finally got there, it was late. As she entered the bedroom, a large rat scampered across the floor. She screamed, "I'm out of here!"

Although rats are not my favorite animal, I was not alarmed and didn't feel any fear. Rats are messengers that show up whenever portals of change are about to enter my life.

As soon as we unpacked, Conrado, the lead dancer, said, "We are going to a festival."

When we got to the festival, I felt I had traveled through a wormhole to another dimension. There was a round raised stage with a Mexican band playing very loud music. In front of a small Catholic church, the Aztec dancers were spinning patterns of energy. The bells were ringing, and chanting could be heard through the doors of the church. The sound was shattering. My ears were hurting, my head was pounding, and I was merging with the chaos.

To save my sanity, I slipped into the church and sat in the back. My heart began to beat at a normal rate and my breathing began to deepen. I did not realize that I had been holding my breath. One of the first things I did in Mexico was to take communion.

At this point I had no idea where Bella was, and I was hungry. As the dancers finished, I said, "I'm really getting hungry. When can we go eat?"

"Don't worry. There is a feast being given by a relative. We can eat there."

Feeling lightheaded from not eating, I felt out of control. This was not anything like my normal everyday life. This was not Florida. I wasn't sure it was even on this planet!

The place where the feast was being held was made up of several two-story houses built around a courtyard. The living spaces were on the second floor. Tables of various sizes and shapes were in the courtyard. Chickens, pigs, and goats were roaming everywhere, including the tops of the tables. Several animals had climbed the steps and were in the kitchen. It was full of woman, children, and animals. I watched the women preparing the food, and knew I could not eat. I asked someone to please take me back to the house, as I was not feeling well.

After I was dropped off, I discovered that all the doors were locked and I could not get into any of the rooms. I was alone and feeling abandoned. My only choice was to sit on the cement alley floor, lean against the stove, and wait until everyone came home. By the time everyone arrived, I was starving! I was grateful that they brought me some bread, which I managed to choke down. My hunger was stronger than the memory of pigs, goats, and chickens.

I was thinking of going to bed, when Conrado said, "My wife has been very sick. The spirits said you could help her."

Thinking he was crazy, "Excuse me!"

"Don't worry, you'll know what to do."

As he put his wife on the bed, he handed me a copper bowl with twigs in it for a fire, and a bottle of alcohol. Around the bowl was a golden light.

I don't know what happened next, but it felt like I was someone else. I knew exactly what to do: how to suck the disease out, how to wash my mouth out with alcohol, how to spit the disease into the fire, and how to pray in Spanish. His wife had a tumor. When the ceremony was done the tumor was gone. I was very aware that I did not do this. My body was being used by a Spirit or another being. I am not a medicine woman. My body was used as a hollow bone.

Very early the next morning, Conrado woke us. "I am ready to leave, but I need a new set of tires." I pulled out my credit card and handed it to him.

The tires were cheaper than the flight we had booked to Palenque. It is common on adventures like this to pay for tires, batteries, food, and rooms for everyone.

Both of us were just beginning to feel awake when we heard, "I forgot, we have to go pick up my uncle." After the tires were changed and paid for, the three of us piled in the car and headed into the unknown.

After traveling for several hours, we arrived at a small village in the hills. I felt like Dorothy in "The Wizard of Oz," and knew this wasn't home.

On either side of a narrow road were houses. Everyone was dressed in white. No one spoke to us. They just watched.

We were introduced to his uncle, Ramon. Later, I found out that he was a *curandero*. A *curandero* is a traditional native healer found primarily in Latin America.

When offered food and drink, it is considered rude and disrespectful not to eat. We were served raw shrimp, some kind of fruit, and Kool-Aid. The travel books warned us about eating these kinds of foods, but I was hungry.

We spent the night, leaving early as the sun rose over the trees. We thought we were headed to Palenque. But the *curandero* had other plans. We headed south towards Veracruz. Conrado smiled, "We are going to a sacred place."

On our way to the sacred site, we drove through the outskirts of Catemaco, a city located inland in southern Veracruz where a number of witches live. As Ramon spoke, there was high tension in his voice, "Drive faster and be very careful!" Just as he finished speaking, a witch flew up in front of the windshield. She pulled up her black skirt and top and displayed her private parts. She was flying backwards. No matter how fast Conrado drove, the witch kept ahead of the car. The *curandero* spoke something and made a sign in the air, and she suddenly just disappeared. Bella and I sat with our mouths open, unable to speak or even laugh.

Just when you think you have seen it all, you often get another surprise. The day was overcast, and we had just missed being witched. I was feeling tired but safe. Bella was napping. As I looked out the window, I saw an alien standing beside the road. He had on a full white mask and appeared green. Then about 50 feet along the road I saw another of these beings. They kept appearing beside the road for about five miles. By now, Bella was awake.

We looked at each other and started laughing again. When things seemed to be outside normal reality, our defense was always, "I'm going to pretend this isn't happening."

* * * *

As we arrived at the sacred site, the air was pulsating with electric energy. In front of us was a Mayan ball court. On each side of the court was carved a stone hoop that the ball passed through. The Maya played with a ball made out of *chicle*, a material extracted from Mesoamerican trees. The ball weighed about 6 to 8 pounds. The players could only touch the ball with their hips, shoulders, knees, and elbows. The game could not be played using feet, hands, or head.

The ball court was built acoustically perfect. A whisper from one end of the court traveled clearly to the other end of the court. The intense sound waves were not affected by climatic conditions, wind direction, or whether it was night or day.

We do not hear sound just with the ears. We hear sound through every molecule of our bodies. It permeates our entire being. It gifts us with the truth of our soul.

History seeped out of the cracks in the stone wall. The colors of the morning painted the eastern sky, rainbow light reflected off low hanging clouds, a mist was rising above the court. As the mist parted to bring a new day, I could see several structures on the hill above us. At the top of the incline, it became clear that these were temples of different religions and beliefs. There were twelve temples.

Spirits, wearing ceremonial garments from a different time, walked among the temples and lush jungle. The air shimmered. Colors swirled and broke apart like shattered glass. Whirlwinds of light particles opened a portal. Love touched all that existed in that moment.

As if he were standing in the presence of sacred beings, the *curandero* spoke softly. "*These temples are the chakras of the Spirit World. They have existed through all Time. Even before the last big destruction. Long ago, we met here and honored each other. These are different paths to remembering our Creator.*" A tear rolled down his cheek.

Although there was great joy in seeing these temples, I felt sadness that the sacred chakras of different beliefs had been forgotten. Could peace across our planet still be remembered and created?

* * * *

We arrived in Palenque and checked into a hotel. Apparently, I had not been careful. The food I ate carried bacteria, probably the shrimp, fruit, or Kool-Aid. Sharp pains tore through my stomach and reminded me of having a baby. I was so sick that the *curandero* offered a healing ceremony.

They pushed all the furniture against the walls, and stood me in the middle of the room. Kerosene was poured in a circle around me and lit. The flames came alive and danced around the circle.

Through my panic, I shouted, "You are going to burn the hotel down, and I am going to have to pay for it." Thank God it was a tile floor!

After dragging me through the flames several times, I collapsed. I was exhausted.

In the middle of the night, Bella got up and turned on the lights. As I opened my eyes, she was dressing in her long white ceremonial dress. It was embroidered with beautiful flowers.

"Where are you going?" I mumbled.

Looking glassy-eyed, she answered, "They are calling me. I have to go."

As she slipped out the door, I went back to bed. I was still too sick to care about anything. What seemed like only a few minutes later, Bella was pounding on the door, "Let me in." There was fear in her voice. Unlocking the door, I quickly opened it. Bella began pushing all the furniture up against the door. "Get your glasses. Look out the window."

About 100 feet from the hotel pool was a shiny saucer-like convex disc. It appeared to be a small spaceship. Exiting the ship were reptilian-like beings. They reminded me of pictures from Egypt. They were walking upright, had short arms, long tails, and squared-off snouts. As they moved away from the craft, they stopped and began to shimmer. When the shimmering stopped, there was a human standing where the alien had been! A few began to clean the pool. Others went into the hotel.

I did not care to scan and investigate whether their intentions were good or bad. I looked at Bella. "We are out of here in the morning."

Very early the next morning, we left the hotel and went to the ancient site of Palenque.

The site was not open to the public for several hours. Ramon talked to the gatekeeper and he let us in early.

The Temple of Inscriptions is Palenque's main attraction, and a masterpiece of architecture. Within the temple is a stairway that leads down to the tomb of Pakal, the king of the Maya around 100 BCE.

As we entered the temple, the lights had not been turned on. When we started down the stairs, they were totally dark. As the *curandero* stepped on each step, it would light up. Taking the last few steps, we arrived at Pakal's tomb. As I stood looking at it, the vibrations of my heart moved like hummingbird wings. A song found life in my voice.

I began to sing. Looking up the stairs we had just come down, I saw Pakal floating towards us. The *curandero* grabbed my arm, "Be careful!"

Just then, the electric lights turned on and the spirit of Pakal disappeared. Dimensions without time wrapped around me. I was there, here, and nowhere.

As we exited the temple, we walked toward the Palace of Palenque. Ramon pointed towards the Observation Tower where we were going to do the ceremony. Bella and I walked ahead. When we got to the steps leading up, we looked back. Ramon and Conrado were talking to the guards near the gate. Ramon had said that we needed to do the ceremony at the top of one of the towers at exactly sunrise.

Bella just shook her head, "If we don't hurry, we will not make it by sunrise." We ran up the stairs. Breathing hard, we reached the top step. To our astonishment, both Ramon and Conrado were standing there. I had recently heard of bi-location, but wasn't sure I believed in it. Now I do!

We climbed the ladder of the four-story Observation Tower. The altar was positioned at an opening facing the sunrise. Just as we were about to begin the ceremony, a man dressed in black leather and motorcycle gear poked his head through the opening. As I glared at him and shook my head "no," he slowly lowered his head and we never saw him again. Focused on the rising of the sun, I didn't have time to ask myself where his motorcycle was, or what he was doing in Palenque.

As the sun hit the altar, we were all transported back in time. This had been our home. The sun touched each of us with rainbow light and connected us to the grid around Earth, offering unconditional love. We had completed our promise.

* * * *

As we explored the rest of the grounds, the *curandero* motioned me to follow him into the jungle. He pointed to steps going down into a buried temple. He called it the Black Panther Temple. As I walked down the steps, I felt myself becoming this sacred being. As I looked at my arms, I saw only black fur. The urge to run and to be free was overwhelming. My name was Power, *Itzamná*. To merge with one of Mother Earth's other beings is to know her.

Palenque was a place of ceremony, bi-location, dimensional shifts, and even transformation. It is both alive and dead. No one lives there, or perhaps they do.

* * * *

As we left and headed back to Mexico City, I was in extreme pain. In desperation, I asked, "What is the matter with me?"

The *curandero* spoke English part of the time, and pretended he did not understand English the rest of the time. This time he answered, "You are giving birth to a cosmic child." Although I asked him, "What does that mean?" he became deaf and dumb.

Several years later, at an indigenous gathering, I met another *curandero*. I asked him the same question.

"Three of you were chosen. You were the one we thought had the best chance of living through it."

Really! Living through what? To this day, I have no idea what they were talking about.

When I am not getting answers, I usually stop asking, and let it go. I don't have the need for all the answers. I know that someday when it is my time to drop my physical robe, I will understand.

* * * *

As we were driving towards Mexico City, I was still feeling miserable. I blurted out, “I just want to sleep in Florida tonight.” Giving me a quirky smile, the *curandero* said, “Don’t worry, you will.”

It was getting late, and Bella and I were both tired. As I looked out the window, I saw a sign that said, “Florida Motel.” Once again, we started laughing. It had become a joke between us to say, “I am going to pretend this isn’t happening.”

The hotel was interesting!! We had rented two rooms. Each room had a carport with blankets hanging in front to hide cars.

Feeling really angry, “If there are mirrors on the ceiling, I am not staying here.” Of course there were. We stayed anyway. Mirrors can be doorways or unwanted openings for Spirits to come through.

All the concepts of what I understood about reality had already been shattered.

When reality shatters, we have an opportunity to walk through new portals.

* * * *

It was our last day in Mexico. Teotihuacán was our last stop. It is about an hour from Mexico City. The Pyramid of the Sun is the largest building in Teotihuacán. Found along the Avenue of the Dead, near the Pyramid of the Moon, it is part of a large complex.

The city of Teotihuacán is astronomically aligned. The Pyramid of the Sun faces the point on the horizon where the sun sets on the equinoxes. The Avenue of the Dead is connected to Pleiades.

As the four of us ascended the Pyramid of the Sun to the platform near the top, it was harder to breathe, and the air smelled different. As we went higher, I could feel different portals opening. I felt myself falling into a different dimension. Bella put her hands up and all three of us began to sing in a language I had never heard. As we sang, a pillar of white light moved from the Sun through Bella and into the pyramid. As the light moved down the avenue of the dead, every temple became covered in Gold.

Everyone on the pyramid sat down on the steps. Sitting a few steps below us were a young father and his son. "Papi, what are those people doing?"

With a look of awe and amazement in his eyes, the father said, "Those are Mayans singing to the Gods."

Wait a minute. Bella had very white skin and long blond hair. My skin was even lighter and was a striking contrast with my red hair. Only Conrado and the *curandero* looked indigenous.

As we walked down the pyramid, the people parted, forming an open path for us to walk through. Some even bowed. What had the young boy and his father seen? What reality were the people imaging?

As Ramon and I walked down the Avenue of the Dead to investigate the other temples and markets, I shared my experience of the Black Panther with him.

I mentioned that I wished I had something to remind me of the experience. He stopped in his tracks, put his hand out, and snapped his fingers. A Black Panther Mayan artifact was sitting in his hand. It had appeared out of thin air. That Black Panther sits center stage on the altar. The panther is a part of me and holds me in protection across all dimensions in the past, present, and future.

Taking my seat on the plane, my mind reviewed everything that had happened. Leaving Mexico, I knew that my past reality had been ripped away. I knew that I was either "certifiably" crazy, or that *reality was beyond imagination.*

Walk gently through
the lives of your ancestors
where time does not exist.
In the stillness of your being
is the center of Creation.

—Grandma Barbara

PERU

I may be part gypsy! I love to travel. My friend Michael Lightweaver announced he was taking a group to Peru; I couldn't pick up the phone fast enough. Michael's knowledge and information of Peru was enormous. He shared that knowledge through dance, storytelling, and channeling.

There was no free ticket this time. I reluctantly sold a few pieces of jewelry, and used the money to book my ticket.

Peru includes part of the Amazon rainforest, as well as Machu Picchu, an ancient Incan city high in the Andes Mountains. Nearby are the Sacred Valley, Inca Trail, Pisac, Cusco, and more archaeological sites.

We landed in Lima, the capital of Peru, and flew on to Cusco. Cusco, a city in the Peruvian Andes, was the capital of the Inca Empire. The ruling emperor was *Pachacuti.* At around 11,000 feet in elevation, it is often called City of the Clouds.

Michael had made arrangements for us to travel with Willaru Huayta. Willaru is known as a *Chasqui*, and a Spiritual Messenger of the Sun. Highly trained and physically fit, the *chasquis* were runners in charge of carrying the messages throughout Inca empire. As a young man, Willaru ran to the different regions announcing the start of *Inti Raymi.* Now he shares spiritual messages from the highest beings.

Willaru is definitely not from this planet. Often his messages are so esoteric that you cannot understand half of what he says.

After some of the group had coca leaf readings by an Inca priest, and explored the markets, we found our way to the ceremony of the *Inti Raymi.*

Inti Raymi is an ancient *Quechua* ceremony celebrated for thousands of years in honor of the Incan Sun deity, *Inti.*

It is filled with rituals and traditions in gratitude for the gift of life. *Inti Raymi* is also the celebration of the winter solstice. Thousands of people gather to plead with the Sun God to return and give life to their crops. Every year, this sacred ceremony is celebrated in Peru as a holy day.

Arriving for the ceremony, we saw an ancient rock amphitheater with a large flat circle below it. In the center of the circle was a stone altar with steps leading up and a small enclosure on top of it. The circular amphitheater was filled with tribes from different regions. They were dressed in the colorful traditional regalia of their individual tribes. Going around the circle, each regional group sang their tribe's sacred song. When they finished, the next tribe would take up the singing. As the sound filled the amphitheater, all the tribes united to sing one sacred song.

As they sang, the song began to fly like the condor. The condor circled the altar and the *Inca* appeared on the causeway.

Young virgins with long hair below their knees flipped their hair, covering the causeway. The *Inca* was being carried in a golden chair by several warriors. As they walked across the virgins' hair, there was a feeling of purity and honor.

Ascending the steps to the altar, the *Inca* held a stone vessel containing the maize drink, *chicha*, as an offering to the Sun God.

A very old llama was led out of the enclosure and its head was lowered onto the altar.

Now, you would think that the llama would cry out, but as he was sacrificed, the llama did not make a single sound. Sacrificing the llama was a gift to the Sun God, as well as to the people. It was holy. It was a sacred and holy prayer.

What surprised me was the rush of emotions. I felt guilt. I felt shame. I felt ecstasy. I felt fear. I felt a connection to the llama and to the Sun God, *Inti*. I felt pure love. All of these emotions rushed in at once. The feeling of ecstasy surprised me the most. I felt unholy.

As a child on the farm, when we butchered the calves and the pigs, I hid under the bed. The *Inti Raymi* taught me that perspective can be different not only in past lives, but in other times of this life and other dimensions of time. The tears were rolling down my face. I was sobbing. I knew that I had lived this before.

* * * *

It was time to leave Cusco, and head to Machu Picchu. We all boarded a bus toward Machu Picchu. Willaru had brought three other priests to travel with us and help with ceremonies.

Apparently, the bus driver was also a very good guide; the priests pointed, and he knew just where to go. We walked up a small mountain. At the top was a circle of standing stones. If you turned in a circle, you could see *Apus* in each of the four directions. An *Apu* is a mountain with a living spirit.

Willaru and the other priests began doing a ceremony. They were singing songs praising the Sun and the *Apus*. Praying, I put my hands towards the sun. As I'm looking at the sun, a laser beam of light came directly from the sun and hit me in the middle of my forehead, the third eye. The third eye is linked to perception, awareness, and spiritual communication.

I fell over backwards and passed out.

Lying on the ground, I became partially conscious. Everyone was leaving. I was aware enough to realize they were stepping on me. I couldn't feel it. But they were stepping on me. They were walking through me. Confused, I thought, "Why don't they walk around me?" Apparently, when I fell over, I became invisible.

Everyone walked away from the ceremonial grounds, got on the bus, and left.

I'm still on the ground thinking, "They're leaving me behind. Why are they doing that?"

About five miles down the road, they finally missed me. By the time they returned for me, I had partially manifested a solid form. But I still couldn't move. Michael Lightweaver and Willaru picked me up and carried me to the bus. It was a full 24 hours before I was completely back in my body.

* * * *

The bus continued towards Machu Picchu. At the foot of the mountain, we stopped to get lunch in the little village of *Aguas Calientes*, the local name for the town of Machu Picchu. The town is located on the banks of the Urubamba River. It is known for its natural hot springs. In the early 1980s, there were only a few buildings, and one small café.

After lunch, some of the women played in a nearby stream. Two teenage boys were laughing and laughing, saying "Piranha, piranha, piranha." I kept telling them to get out, but they still had small ears. Maybe those piranha had a good lunch!

Arriving at the ruins, we checked into our hotel. At the time, it was the only hotel and had only eight rooms. I immediately headed for the site. Walking around the grounds, I kept seeing balls of light, or *orbs,* floating in the air. There were more of them at the temples and on the stairs connecting the temples. I saw beautiful women dressed in white walking throughout the site. These were not tourists.

The first ceremony that we did was at a large stone altar to *Pachamama,* the Earth Mother. *Pachamama* has long been one of the most revered deities among the indigenous people of the Andes. She is the goddess with the power to give and sustain life. She is present in every mountain. She rules over all the plant life on Earth.

During an hour-long ceremony, we presented small gifts to *Pachamama,* including flowers, grains, herbs, coca leaves, alcohol, and candles. The aromas and beauty of these gifts carried the prayers. The belief is that people must nurture *Pachamama* with good food, including beans and potatoes. We asked for her blessings of health and prosperity, and the powerful natural energy of well being. I felt that I was being held and loved by my Mother. All my life I had craved this love.

When I'm preparing for a trip, Spirit will tell me to pack items that make no sense. I don't question, I just pack them. Before I left for Peru, Spirit told me to bring a silver Mylar blanket that is used when you're really cold. They had me cut a neck hole into it and sew on sleeves, so it looked like a shiny sweat dress.

Michael Lightweaver was at another holy area channeling *Quetzalcoatl*. Because I'd heard him so many times before, I chose to see what else was around. I noticed a line of standing stones. I put on the Mylar dress, stepped up on one of the stones' platforms, and leaned against the rocks.

I immediately disappeared again. It seemed like disappearing was becoming a habit. The rock was a portal that briefly took me home. I traveled through all of Creation until I came to this planet where I started life. Gravity pulled me to its center core where fire ignited the knowledge of Creation.

Having disappeared again, no one noticed that I was missing. I'm left there floating around in the universe seeing marvelous things. At the time, I was having a real issue with why all the religions in the world are led by men. The prayers were always to "our father." The spirits took me to the place where Cosmic Mother and Cosmic Father were hanging out. Cosmic Mother was breathing in and out, and with every exhale, she breathed out a soul. Cosmic Father blew on them, and gave them a form that could be incarnated.

Even though Cosmic Mother held the whole secret of birthing a soul, the Cosmic Father could manifest any soul into solid form, or manifest any religious idea.

At this point, I stopped having problems with religions being led only by men. I understood the balance.

The group had already gone back to the hotel, but I'm still trapped on this rock. I felt like I had become the rock. I was very cold. I was grateful for the Mylar dress.

Around four o'clock in the morning, the group missed me and came looking. Approaching me a bit frustrated and angry, "What are you still doing here? You need to come back to the hotel."

I had materialized again, but was not quite there and still stuck to the stone. They literally had to peel me off. Once they carried me down to the hotel, I got a couple hours sleep.

* * * *

The next morning at Machu Picchu, Michael introduced me to a guide and archaeologist. There was an immediate recognition. Nine lifetimes ago we had known each other. We walked hand in hand and remembered our love. We had not been able to be together when we were at Machu Picchu. I was a virgin priestess. He was a servant that cared for the priestesses. It was a sacred remembering.

Sometimes you meet someone from a past life, you touch, and reality disappears. When this happens, there's nothing but a white mist. There are no solid objects. Just two souls touching.

* * * *

Mateo taught me the real history of Machu Picchu. He explained that Machu Picchu was not what other archaeologists were claiming. Machu Picchu was a Pleiadian outpost and university. It was like a temple of *Isis*. The women who lived there were Virgins of the Sun.

We walked throughout the ruins. We came to a rock that archaeologists call the Eagle Rock. Their theory is that it was for sacrifices. Instead, Mateo shared with me that directly underneath the Eagle Rock, there was a cave and an altar. A crystal skull sat on the altar. It was pouring down rain, so it was not safe for us to physically go into the cave. Mateo teleported us into the cave. Reading the history written on the walls and watching the spirit beings floating through the darkness, I knew that what he shared was truth. I knew that I was looking at one of the thirteen skulls. It was created, not carved. I don't know whether the crystal skull is still there or not.

Mateo pointed out a flat rock that was about the size of a queen bed. Mateo shared that an honored priestess would lie down on the rock. A Pleiadian would materialize and they would mate. The Pleiadians were developing several outposts in sacred places all over the planet where they created half-Pleiadian beings. When the Spanish came to kill everyone at Machu Picchu, ships arrived from the Pleiades and took us home.

As we left Machu Picchu, I was overcome with sadness. I knew I would not be back, and I knew that on this dimension I would not see Mateo again.

Joy filled my being as I remembered there is no time and space.

All dimensions exist simultaneously.

Reality is an
ever-changing perception
without limits.
It only takes one small step
to remember.
You are the DreamTime.

—Grandma Barbara

AUSTRALIA

Just when you think that you have shared all that needs to be shared, Spirit steps in and says, "You are not done."

Most of the time I do not argue with Spirit, although I admit that this time I tried. Spirit let me know that my ears were still small.

As one of the Peace Elders traveling to many different countries doing ceremony and sharing the teachings of our ancestors, in 1993 we were invited to Australia to gather with indigenous Aboriginal elders and others from around the world. The gathering was called *A World Peace Council of Indigenous Elders*, or *Jinta Jungu*, meaning *Together as One*.

I always travel with someone who keeps me grounded. This time it was my friend Gail, who had studied with *Beautiful Painted Arrow*. Gail was well trained in how sound creates reality. We had spent many hours together sharing ancestral teachings. She knew how to behave and to protect me.

Traveling to Australia is not going down the street to the grocery store. First, it was a sixteen-hour trip. Second, the organizers forgot to meet us at the airport. Third, Gail and I did not know where we were to go. People think that when difficulties start happening, it means they should not do what Spirit asks them to do. I have found that there are some forces that take pleasure in preventing us from growing and healing. They do not want us to walk in love.

When I got there I was exhausted. Everything was upside down. The stars were spinning away from me, causing intense nausea. My stomach felt like it had been punched, and I was rapidly being pulled into a black hole.

Adding to this feeling of being in an unknown reality, a New Zealand elder, *Rangimarie Rose Turuki Pere*, showed up. She was wearing a wild, flowered dress, a big hat with an artificial red rose on it, and bedroom slippers. Let me remind you that the Universe has a sense of humor. *Rose* looked just like my mother. Old emotions from my childhood rocketed to the surface. At that moment fear, shame, guilt, and trauma took over my brain. My heart sank. Confidence was sucked out of me. Just looking at her triggered childhood memories. Here I was at a gathering of indigenous Peace Elders, acting like a child. *Rose* gifted me with the opportunity to know that:

I am enough.

* * * *

Finally arriving at the gathering, we were greeted by *Mary Thunder.* The first day we were on our own.

Many of us went to a reserve that protected kangaroos. There was a colony of them gathered in an open area. A large male was obviously in charge. We had been told not to take pictures. There were a number of tourists from another country that had not gotten the memo. Cameras aimed at the females were flashing every second. Each time a flash went off, the kangaroos would flinch. I watched as the male became agitated. All of a sudden he kicked one of the tourists, and sent the camera flying. As it hit the ground, he used his tail to smash it into small pieces.

Feeling the intense emotions, I moved away. If there ever was proof that animals feel emotions of anger and fear, this was it. I realized that we are more similar to our animal brothers and sisters than different. Aren't we just animals with egos?

Not wanting to be in the middle of this fight between the kangaroo and the tourists, I found a bench and sat down. Taking a beet and mayo sandwich out of my pocket, I began to eat. A female *roo* approached. I offered her a small piece of my sandwich. Continuing to give her small pieces, she nudged my hand, and glanced at her pouch. Watching her do this several times, I put my hand towards the pouch. Using her nose, she moved my hand so that it slid into the pouch. Touching the inner lining of the pouch, I felt a tiny *joey*, about an inch long. Holding it gently, I was overcome with gratitude and honor. I could feel its tiny heart beating and its intent to live. Connecting with this small being opened my heart. It is the heart that reaches the soul of an animal. I had received the gift of absolute trust from this mother. When trust is present, souls connect.

On the way back, we spotted a small takeout serving fish and chips. Beet sandwiches were not my favorite food.

* * * *

Arriving back at the gathering, I walked around, introducing myself to other elders. One particular Aboriginal elder intrigued me. *Guboo* was small for an Aboriginal. Yet the power he carried spoke of dimensions I was not familiar with. He walked the *DreamTime.*

According to many Aboriginal stories, *DreamTime* is the time when all life was created. These stories date back some 65,000 years. The stories explain how the universe and human beings were created, and how they are to live within this world. During the *DreamTime*, the land, mountains, rivers, plants, animals, humans, including the star nations, were created.

DreamTime is the continuum of past, present and future. Aboriginal people understand that the *DreamTime* is a beginning that never ended. It is a way to live.

* * * *

The gathering was in *Yuin* country on the southeast coast near the ocean. As *Guboo*, the Yuin lore man, walked towards the beach, he invited me and Evie, one of his students, to join him. Evie would become my star sister. Just as we arrived, he handed me two clap sticks. Clap sticks, or *Bilma*, are a traditional instrument. They serve to hold the rhythm of dances and voice chants in ceremony. *Guboo* showed me how to match the beat of the clap sticks to the heartbeat of Mother Earth. The sound touched everything. It invaded my heart, and activated the memory of being in a womb. This time it was the womb of Mother Earth. I became her child, suckling at her breast. She was my real Mother. I had always been loved.

Standing in the morning sunlight, *Guboo* began to sing. As the water shimmered and splashed on the shore, it sounded like a water drum. Arising out of the water, a pod of dolphins greeted the elder. They smiled and splashed water on both of us. As they communicated, I knew I was in the presence of those that also held the *DreamTime*.

Walking back towards the main area, another Aboriginal knowledge keeper invited me to go for a short walkabout. As we followed a path through the woods, I saw several brightly colored snakes. He spoke, "In Australia we have more poisonous snakes than anywhere else in the world."

Several indigenous cultures speak of snakes as a symbol for transformation of the old, and fresh beginnings. All I could think about was that I was not ready to die.

* * * *

The registration table had been set up and everything was ready to go. It was a small gathering with a very low budget, especially for food. One of the girls taking tickets came to *Thunder* and told her that more people had tickets than we had food for. It seemed like someone bought one ticket and printed many copies.

When we realized there were more people than we could feed, I went to the cooks and told them the stories of Grandpa Dubray and Christ both making a little food feed multitudes.

Grandpa said, “That one I walk with, he said greater things than I do you can do.”

I asked them to pray for all the people, to ask that there be enough food, and to put love and light into the food.

Among those eating was a shriveled up old man dressed in black. He appeared somewhat crippled. He had very long fingernails and his hands were contorted with pain.

Beside him was a red-haired woman wearing a bright red see-through top that showed everything except what the pockets covered. She had on an extremely short skirt and sat in a very provocative posture.

They appeared very demonic. Instead of white light surrounding them, the light was black. Several of the Elders became very frightened. *Guboo* even mentioned there were negative energies to be dealt with. One of the Elders was so frightened, she left to return home, saying, "I'm out of here."

As I glanced in their direction, they challenged me by staring directly into my eyes. Shivers went up and down my spine.

Several young people appeared to be his followers. They were there to stop the gathering, try to harm us, deplete our food, and be initiated.

After everyone had eaten, I walked to the front of the food tent and asked *Thunder* for permission to speak. "I know that some of you came here to disrupt this gathering and to harm some of us. I want you to know that you are in deep doo-doo. The food that you just ate was filled with love and light. Enjoy what you're going to experience."

Thunder shook her head, "Oh my God, you did not just say that!"

From that moment on, every place I sat, the demonic leader and his woman sat behind me. Although their energy felt dark and menacing, I knew that Gail, Spirit, and the Elders had my back.

* * * *

We were called to the circle to hear the wisdom of all the different indigenous Elders.

When going to Australia, it is the custom to be welcomed to a country by a senior lore man and senior lore woman. As the gathering was being held in Yuin country, *Guboo Ted Thomas* and his niece *Mary Duroux* were the Yuin Elders who welcomed us.

This is done by offering prayers asking the land of the ancestors to watch over the people and keep the guests safe while they're in the country.

The senior Yuin also talks to the ancestors, promising to look after the guests while they are in the country, and to return them safely to their own country.

When Aboriginals talk about country, it has a sacred meaning. This connection means more than just the land or waters. There is no English word that gives meaning or understanding of how this reaches into their culture, spirituality, language, law, family, and the land. It provides a deep sense of identity, purpose, and belonging.

* * * *

After being welcomed to Australia by the Yuin elders, the Maori Elders began their ritual. When the Maori of New Zealand meet strangers, they also do a ceremony. The ceremony originated when the Maori were warring tribes. It is called the *Haka*, a ceremonial dance of challenge. It was done to show their strength and unity.

Wiremu Pounamu Poutapu Korako Ruka, referred to as *Grandfather Macki*, tattooed with sacred symbols, assumed an intimidating stance. Stomping his feet, pounding his chest, contorting his face, bulging his eyes, protruding his tongue, rhythmically slapping his body, and fiercely yelling a chant of challenge. At that moment, he was a Maori warrior welcoming us. At the same time, he was letting us know not to mess with him or his people.

As he dropped a sacred object on the ground, *Thunder*, never losing eye contact, reached out and picked it up, proving her courage.

I was certainly feeling intimidated.

Although the *Haka* required direct eye contact, in many indigenous cultures this is considered rude. Depending on the culture, it is appropriate to either lower your eyes or look over the person's shoulder when you speak to them. Many cultures believe that the eyes are a window to the soul. By looking directly in someone's eyes you could steal their soul.

* * * *

Rangimarie Rose Turuki Pere, referred to as *Grandma Rose* had been standing behind *Macki* holding space. It was her time to step forward.

Grandma Rose raised her voice to the people, "In my language, we have a word '*aroha*' which means the presence and the breadth of our Divine source, which is love. Love that is never-ending."

She put her hands towards the sun and a song began to sing her.

Until a woman's song creates a sacred space, nothing else can happen. The Song welcomed not only the people, but all their ancestors.

Aio ki te Aorangi
{Peace, Peace, Peace to the Universe}

Aroha ki te Aorangi
{Love, Love, Love to the Universe}

Koa, koa, koa ki te Aorangi
{Joy, Joy, Joy to the Universe}

Pono ki te Aorangi
{Truth, Truth, Truth to the Universe}

Her voice sent a shiver up and down my spine. Although the Maori words were unfamiliar, I knew she was weaving a sacred portal.

* * * *

Time to exhale for a minute. Here is a funny story about *Grandfather Macki Ruka.* A few years later, *Macki* came to the United States. At this time, *Macki* weighed around 400 pounds. We were staying in a house with a steep staircase; *Macki* was sleeping upstairs. I was sound asleep downstairs on the couch deep in *DreamTime.*

In the middle of the night, I could hear *Macki* coming down the stairs. He moved towards the couch and sat on my chest.

"*Macki*, get off of me. I can't breathe." He had squished me.

"I'm sorry sister, but I need your help. I've taught all these women to eat for me when I am fasting, and send me the energy of the food. Now they send me that food all the time. Look what is happening to me."

Still trying to get my breathing back to normal, I said, "*Macki*, tell them to ask permission before they eat for you and send you the energy."

Watching what was happening to *Macki* taught me to always ask permission before you pray for someone or send them energy. It is important to ask them what they want you to pray for, and if they will accept the responsibility for the changes the prayers will bring to their life. The only friends I ask to pray for me are those that focus on the body remembering its perfection as *Tȟuŋkášila*, God, created it.

When we ask for prayers, people often focus on the illness or problem. That gives it power. It may even make you or them sicker, and certainly won't solve the problem.

When you are praying for someone, if you do not understand how to protect yourself, there is the possibility that you will take on their illness. I remember Grandpa saying to me, "Don't let them kill you."

* * * *

One of the highlights of the gathering was the female Aboriginal dancers. They wore short black skirts and were topless. Their feet stamped in rhythm with the clapping sticks. As their movement mirrored the spiral of *DreamTime*, each of us fell into a hologram, collapsing time and space. A rainbow appeared connecting the people to the ancestors of the land. The ancestors moved with the dancers.

Songs of *DreamTime* reminded us that *Here* was not *Reality*.

My whole being expanded as I understood that *Everything* that Happens in all of Creation is connected.

* * * *

We had been told not to touch the Aboriginals. I was sitting in the circle next to *Mary Duroux*, known as *Aunt Mary*. She reached over, put her hand on my knee, "You come back and I will teach you."

I never made it back.

* * * *

Later that evening, I was asked to perform a traditional Celtic ceremony. The Celts were people indigenous to Northern Europe and Ireland. They believed they came to Earth on ships from another galaxy. They are my ancestors.

Traditional Celts understood the number three as representing the three realities of all existence: Spiritual, Earth, and the Underworld where fairies and the ancestors existed. The number three also represents the sky, land, and sea. The elements represented in their ceremonies are: fire, earth, and water. Stones and rocks are the knowledge holders. The ancient Celts were deeply connected to nature and believed that trees were portals to the spirit world.

The objects used in ceremonies are an apple, bread, a staff, wine, fire, water, and the Dragons. When an apple is cut in half, there is a star that reminds us that we came from the stars. The bread feeds the ancestors. The staff is a tool of power that connects Earth and Sky. Wine represents the Dragon's blood. Many indigenous peoples have animals that are sacred to them, such as the Thunderbird, the Eagle, and the Condor. Celtics have their Dragons.

As we gathered for the ceremony, I placed a star dome of protection around the ceremonial circle. I sealed it except for a small hole in the top of the dome for the full moon to shine through. The full moon's energy was needed for the ceremony. I called in the Dragons. A portal opened to the past.

Just as the energy reached its peak, a small stone was thrown through the hole in the top of the protective shield. As the stone hit me, it was like being struck by lightning. I smelled sulfur burning. My ears were ringing, I went numb and my whole body just stopped. I couldn't move. I collapsed onto the ground.

The energy was meant to kill me, or at least stop me. After checking that Gail and everyone else were still alive, I reached down and picked the stone up. Wrapping it in one of the Celtic shawls, I asked Gail to take it to the water and ask that the water and dolphins clear it of any harmful energies.

I immediately became very sick. I was carried to the room that Gail and I were staying in. I was sick for several hours. My temperature was 102. Black stuff kept coming out of my mouth. I had visions of negative things happening to each elder.

Although still sick, we were approached by a young woman who told us she no longer wanted to be a part of the demonic group. She said they were disruptive and harmful. Could we help her?

Gail did a clearing ceremony with her, and she seemed fine. I was too sick to help. The next morning I saw her again. She was wearing some demonic symbols, and I realized that she must have been an initiate and her challenge was to resist the unconditional love we offered her.

As I left Australia, I thought about the fact that I had gone there to teach. Instead, I had become the student.

I met the caretakers of the *DreamTime.* I learned: to stay humble, there is always more to learn, and no matter how much we think we know, we are still vulnerable.

The ego can get you killed.

I will always be with you.
You can always find me
where you find
Love.

—Grandma Blue Star